no	**Is this a pin?** yes no
yes	**Is it a pig?** yes no
no	**Is the pig tan?** yes no
pan	**This pig is in a** pin. pan.
p<u>i</u>g	**This is a p___g in a pan.**
pig	**Sam has a** pig. pin.
pi<u>n</u>	**Ann has a pi___.**
pin	**This man has a pig and a** pin. pan.
pin	**The** pin pig **is in his hand.**
pi<u>g</u>	**The pi___ is tan.**

1

	This is Nip.
no	Is Nip a pig? yes / no
no	Is this Nip? yes / no
Th<u>i</u>s	Th___s is Tab.
no	Is Tab a pig? yes / no
cat	Tab is a cat. / can.
no	Is this Nip? yes / no
no	Is it Tab? yes / no
yes	Is it a pig? yes / no
Nip	Sam has Nip. / Tab.
T<u>a</u>b	Ann has T___b.
ca<u>t</u>	Tab is Ann's ca___.

2

p̲ig	A pig can dig. This __ig is digging.
di̲g yes	Nip can d__g. Can Tab dig? yes no

yes
 	
yes
 	
d̲ig
	Can Sam dig? yes
	          no
	
	Can Ann dig? yes
	          no
	
	Sam and Ann can __ig.

yes di̲g	Is this pig digging? yes no A pig can di__.

3

no	Is Ann digging? yes / no
<u>d</u>igging	Sam is __igging.
sitting	Ann is sitting. / singing.
napping	The pig is digging. / napping.
digging	The man is singing. / digging.
yes	Is Nip digging? yes / no
yes	Is Tab digging? yes / no
diggi<u>ng</u>	Nip is digging, and Tab is diggi___ .
singing	This man is singing. / digging.

pig	A ^{pin} A _{pig} can dig.
pi<u>g</u>	This pi___ is digging.
no	Is this pig in a pan? ^{yes} _{no}
<u>p</u>ig	The ___ig is in the sand.
Sa<u>m</u>	Sa___ is in the sand.
yes	Is Ann in the sand? ^{yes} _{no}
hand	Sam has sand in his ^{ham.} _{hand.}
pig tan	The sand is ^{tin.} _{tan.}

5

tan	That ant is tin. tan.
yes	Is the ant in the sand? yes no
s<u>a</u>nd	The s___nd is tan.
sand	This pig is in the sand. hand.
pi<u>g</u>	The pi___ digs in the sand.
digs	Sam sits in the sand. digs
<u>s</u>and	Nip naps in the ___and.
s<u>a</u>nd	That is a dish in the s___nd.
di<u>sh</u>	That is a fish in the di___ ___.
sand	The dish is tan. sand

6

yes	Is that a pan in the sand? yes no
sa<u>nd</u>	The sa____ is tan.
no	Is this pan in the sand? yes no
yes	Is Nip in the sand? yes no
<u>s</u>and	That fish is in the ___and.
<u>f</u>ish	Nip sniffs the ___ish.
no	Is Tab in the sand? yes no
ham	Tab has a hat. ham.
ha<u>m</u>	Tab sniffs the ha___.

7

hand	Nip sniffs Sam's hand. sand.
_s_and	Tab sniffs in the ___and.
fish	This man has a dish. fish.
fi_sh_	A cat sniffs the fi___ ___.
dish	Nip has his dish. fish.
d_ish_	Nip sniffs the d___ ___ ___.

8

sits	Tab <u>sits</u> / sniffs in Nip's dish. 
fits	Tab <u>fits</u> / hits in the dish.
can	That is a fish in the <u>can.</u> / pan.
sn<u>i</u>ffs	A cat sn__ffs the fish.
<u>s</u>niffing	Sniff, sniff. Ann is ___niffing.
yes	Is Ann sad? <u>yes</u> / no
<u>s</u>niffs	Nip ___niffs a ham.
<u>sn</u>iffs	Tab ___ ___iffs a fish.

9

hand	Sam has Miss Pat in his hand. / sand.
sits	Miss Pat sits / sniffs in his hand.
This	Th___s is Miss Ant.
hat	Miss Ant has on a hat. / ham.
Miss	Mi___ ___ Ant is tan.
Ant	Tab sniffs Miss A___ ___ .
hid	Miss Ant hit / hid in the sand.
sand	That is Miss Ant in the s___nd.

10

pig	
p**i**g	
hid	
hand	
sn**iff**s	
pi**g**	
fi**sh**	

This man has a pin.
pig.

His p____g is fat.

The pig hit in the sand.
hid

The man has a fish
hand.
in his
sand.

The pig sn____ffs the fish.

The man has his pi____.

The pig has the fi_____.

11

yes	This is a bag. Is it tan? yes no

pig
 	
pig
	That is a pin in the bag.
	        pig
	
	The pig is tan.
	    bag

pan
 	
b**a**g
 	
Sam's
	Ann has a pan.
	         bag.
	
	Sam has a b___g.
	
	The bag is in Ann's hand.
	           Sam's

sa**nd** ba**g**	This bag has sa___ ___ in it. That is sand in the ba___.

12

This is the sandman.

Is the sandman a sad man?
yes
no

no

Is this the sandman?
yes
no

no

This is the s___ndman.

The sandman has a
bag.
pan.

The bag has ___and in it.

s<u>a</u>ndman

bag

<u>s</u>and

Is this the sandman?
yes
no

Is this a sad man?
yes
no

no

yes

13

bag	This is the sandman's bag. / hat.
sand	His bag has ants / sand in it.
<u>s</u>and	The sandman has __and in his hand.
yes	Is Ann napping? yes / no
yes	Is Tab napping? yes / no
no	Is the sandman napping? yes / no
T<u>a</u>b	T__b had a nap.
n<u>a</u>p	Ann had a n__p.

yes	
ba_g_	

Is this a bag? yes
no

It is a big b___g.

bag	
pan	
yes	

Sam has a big bag.
pan.

Ann has a pin.
pan.

Is the pan big? yes
no

b_a_g	
ba_g_	
no	

Ann has a big b___g.

Sam has a tan ba___.

Is the tan bag big? yes
no

bag	
ba_g_	
_s_and	

This is the sandman's bag.
mat.

His b_____ is big.

It has ___and in it.

15

no	Is this a bag? yes / no This is a bat. Is it tan? yes / no
yes	
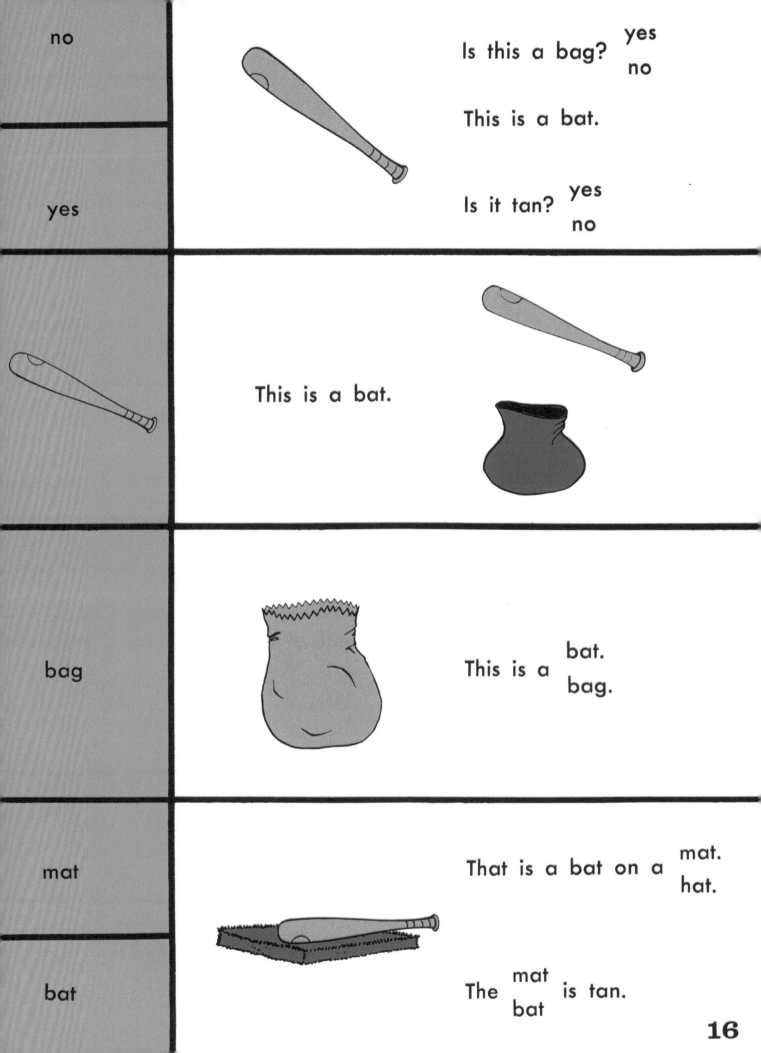	This is a bat.
bag	This is a bat. / bag.
mat	That is a bat on a mat. / hat.
bat	The mat / bat is tan.

16

bat	Sam has a cat. bat.
hands	The bat is in his hat. hands.
bat	Nip has Sam's bat. bag.
b<u>a</u>t	That b___t is Sam's.
bat	Ann has Sam's hat. bat.
hat	Sam has Ann's hat. ham.
h<u>a</u>t	Sam hands Ann the h___t.
<u>b</u>at	Ann hands Sam his ___at.

17

pig	
p**ig**	

This is a   pin.
              pig.

It is a big p＿＿＿.

pin
p**in**

Ann has a   pin.
              pan.

It is a big p＿＿＿.

bag
ba**g**

Sam has a   bat.
              bag.

It is a big ba＿＿.

bat
no

Sam has a big   bat.
                  cat.

Is Ann's bat big?   yes
                      no

18

bat	Ann has a hat and a bat. / bag.
hat	The hat / bat is tan.
bat	Sam has a bag and a cat. / bat.
ba<u>t</u>	The ba___ is tan.
s<u>and</u>	The tan bag has s___ ___ ___ in it.
<u>b</u>ag	A pig is in the big ___ag.
no	Is the big bag tan? yes / no
bag	Tab sniffs a bag. / bat.
b<u>at</u>	Nip sniffs a b___ ___ .
b<u>a</u>g	That is a fish in the b___g.

19

h**i**d	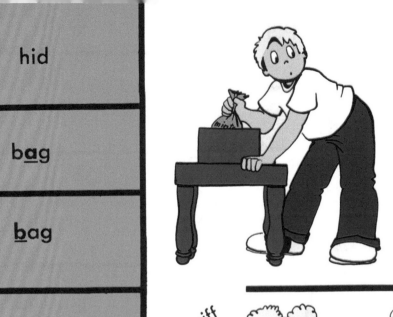 Sam hit / hid a tan bag.
b**a**g	The b___g is Ann's.
bag	The ___ag has mints in it.
sn**i**ffs	 Nip sn___ffs the bag and the mints.
bag	 Nip has Ann's tan bag. / bat.
p**a**ts	Ann bats / pats Nip.
bag	 Ann has the ___ag.
m**i**nt	Nip has a m___nt.

20

ham	
ham	
h**a**m	
yes	
ha**m**	
hid	
h**am**	
Tab	

Ann has a big ham.
                 hat.

Tab sniffs the ___am.

Tab hid the h___m.

Did Nip sniff the ham? yes
                         no

That is Ann's ha___.

Tab hid it.
    hit

Sam has the h___ ___.

Nip hid in a can.
Tab

21

bat		Nip bit a bat. hat.
bit		Tab bit hit a fish.
hit		A fish hit bit Tab.
bat		Sam has a big bat. bit.
hit		Sam hit bit a can.

22

pig	
fat	
bit	
hid	
bag	
ba<u>g</u>	
big	

This is a pin.
pig.

It is thin.
fat.

Nip bit the pig.
hit

The pig hit.
hid.

It hid in a bat.
bag.

The pig fits in the ba___.

The bag is big.
sad.

23

yes	Can a pig dig? yes / no
pig	The pig / cat is digging.
no	Is the cat digging? yes / no
pig	The cat / pig is fat.
thin	The cat is tin. / thin.
bat	The bag / bat is tan.
big	The bag is big. / pig.
no	Is the big bag tan? yes / no
big	That is sand in the bi___ bag.
bag	The cat is in the tan ba___.

24

hit	 Ann hit / bit a bag.
bit	Nip hit / bit a bag.
sits	Ann hits / sits in the sand.
<u>s</u>and	Sam digs in the s_____.
Ann	 Sam / Ann has the big pan.
no	Is the big pan tan? yes / no
<u>t</u>an	Sam has the __an pan.

25

no	
yes	
sh<u>i</u>p	
fast	
no	
f<u>a</u>t	
fat	
no	
no	
no	
bat	
bag	

Is this a dish?   yes
                  no

Is it a ship?   yes
                no

It is a fast sh____p.

The tan cat is   fat.
                 fast.

Is the big cat fast?   yes
                       no

The big cat is f____t.

The big fish is   fat.
                  tan.

Is the tan fish big?   yes
                       no

Is the big fish tan?   yes
                       no

Is the bag on the mat?   yes
                         no

The   bat   is on the mat.
      hat

The   bat   is tan.
      bag

26

bit	 Nip bit / hit that man.
hid	Tab hid / hit in the hat.
sand	Sam and Ann sat in the hand. / sand.
hat	Ann has on a hat. / bat.
bat	That is Sam's bat. / bag.
yes	 Is it in the sand? yes / no
sand	The bat is in the __and.

hand	
hand	This is Sam's hand. / sand.
a**nt**	Sam has an ant in his ___and.
	The a_____ is tan.
yes	Is Nip sitting? yes / no
yes	Is Nip panting? yes / no
s**i**t	Nip can s___t.
pant	Nip can ___ant.
yes	Is Ann sitting? yes / no
yes	Is Ann singing? yes / no
sing**ing**	Ann is sitting and singi_____.
yes	Is Sam patting Nip? yes / no
yes	Is Sam patting Tab? yes / no
patt**ing**	Sam is patt_____ Nip and Tab.

28

no	Is Nip panting? yes / no
yes	Is Nip sniffing? yes / no
sn<u>i</u>ffs	Nip sn___ffs in the sand.
sni<u>ff</u>ing	Tab is sitting. / sniffing.
<u>s</u>niffs	Tab ___niffs a fish.
<u>sn</u>iffs	Nip _____iffs Tab's dish.
sni<u>ff</u>	Nip and Tab sni_____ in the sand.

no	
ba**g**	
b**ag**	

Is that a pig in the bag? yes
no

That is Ann in the ba___.

It is a big b_____ .

bag	
bag	

The sandman has a ___ag.

His _____ has sand in it.

sa**nd**	
digging	

Nip can dig in the sa_____ .

Nip is sitting.
digging.

yes	
digging	

Can this man dig? yes
no

The man is ___igging.

30

pan		Sam can stand on a pan. pat.
yes		Can Ann stand on a pan? yes no
p**an**		Ann stands on a p____.
mat		Nip stands on his mat. map.
hands		Sam can stand on his sands. hands.

31

yes	Is that Ann in the sand? yes / no
sa<u>nd</u>	Ann can stand in the sa _____ .
mat	That is a man on a hat. / mat.
m<u>an</u>	A m _____ can stand on a mat.
pan	A pig can stand on a pat. / pan.
st<u>a</u>nd	A cat can st _____ nd on a can.
<u>st</u>and	A man can _____ tand on a mat.
yes	Can a man stand on his hands? yes / no
<u>st</u>ands	This man _____ ands on his hands.

32

sits	
st**a**nds	

Nip sits / stands on his mat.

Tab st __ nds in the sand.

Ann	
st**a**nding	

Sam / Ann is sitting.

Sam is st __ nding.

pan	
standing	

The pig is standing on a pan. / can.

The cat is __ __ anding on a can.

h**a**nds	
standi**ng**	
sitting	
standi**ng**	

Sam is standing on his h __ nds.

Nip is standi __ __ in the sand.

Tab is sitting. / standing.

Ann is stand__ __ __. **33**

yes	Is this pig standing? yes / no
no	Is it standing on the can? yes / no
sniffing	It is sniffing / hitting the can.
standing	Tab is sitting. / standing.
standing	Tab is ___ ___anding on a can.
handing	Ann is handing / standing Sam a bag.
stand**ing**	Sam is stand_____ in the sand.
handi**ng**	Sam is handi ___ ___ Ann a mint.
sitt**ing**	Ann is sitt___ ___ ___ in the sand.
yes	Is Sam standing? yes / no **34**

sand	That is Sam in the sand. / hand.
	Can Sam stand in the sand? yes / no
yes	
stands	Ann sits / stands on Sam.
no	Is Nip sitting? yes / no
standing.	Nip is standi___.
Ann	Nip sits on Sam. / Ann.
sand	Sam is in the s___nd.
no	Is Tab standing on Sam? yes / no
stands	Tab st___nds on Nip.
no	Is Sam standing? yes / no

35

TEST 1

Is this the sandman? yes

no

The sandman has a bag.
bat.

The bag has s___nd in it.

Is this Sam? yes

no

This is A___.

Ann is standing.
sitting.

Ann is standing and singi___.

Is Tab digging? yes

no

Tab is napping.
panting.

Nip is singing.
digging.

Is this a pig? yes

no

The pig is sniffing.

digging.

A pig can d___g.

36

<u>h</u>and	
sitting	 Ann is standing on Sam's __and. Sam is sitting. standing.
yes	
yes	Is Sam sad? yes no Did Ann stand on his hand? yes no
sits	Sam sits stands on his hands.
s<u>a</u>d	 Ann is s__d.

Nip	
sitting	
hit	
no	
hid	
no	
bit	
yes	

Nip
Tab bit that man.

sitting.
Tab is standing.

The man hit Nip.
bit

Is Tab sitting? yes
no

hid
Nip hit in a bag.

Is Tab in the bag? yes
no

This is the man that Nip hit.
bit.

Did this man hit Nip? yes
no

no	
napping	
mat	
standing	
st**a**nding	
bag	
hit	
s**a**nd	
dish	

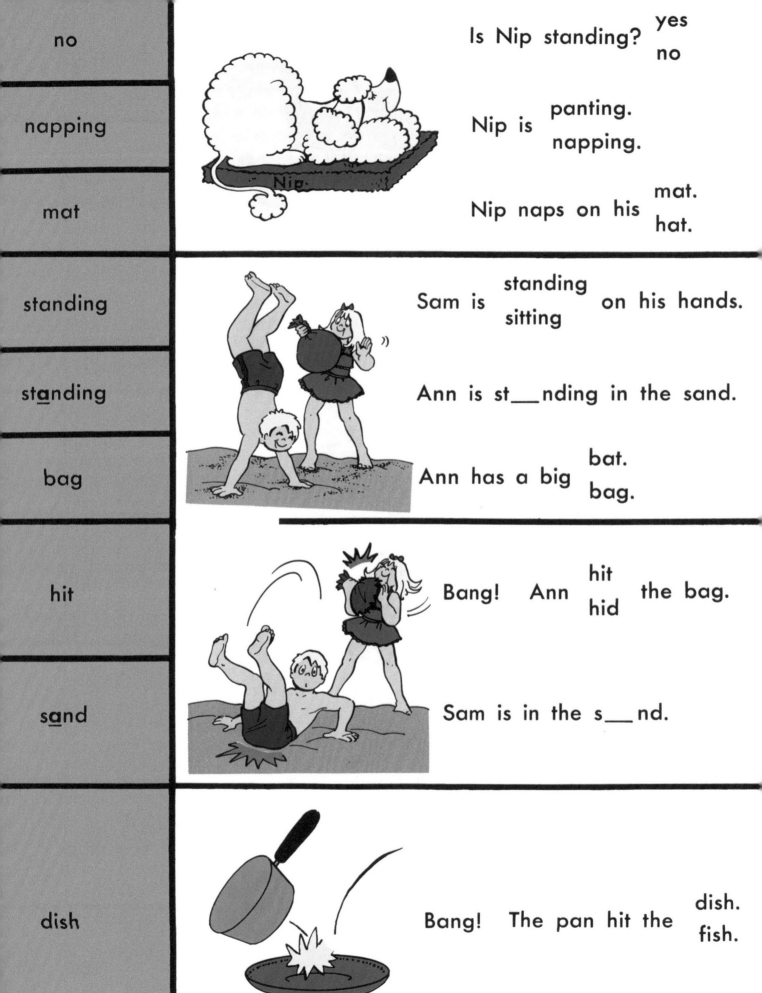

Is Nip standing? yes
no

Nip is panting.
napping.

Nip naps on his mat.
hat.

Sam is standing
sitting on his hands.

Ann is st___nding in the sand.

Ann has a big bat.
bag.

Bang! Ann hit
hid the bag.

Sam is in the s___nd.

Bang! The pan hit the dish.
fish.

39

pan	 Bang, bang! Ann bangs on a pan. fan.
can	 Sam bangs on a cat. can.
bangs	 Bang, bang! The man b___ngs the pans.
no	 Is Ann banging the pans? yes no
bangs	Sam ___angs the pans.

40

yes	
m**an**	

Is this a man? yes
          no

This m___ ___ is in a band.

band

This is a bat.
          band.

yes
b**an**d

Is this a band? yes
              no

Sam is in the b___nd.

no
yes
b**an**d

Is that Sam in the band? yes
                     no

Is it Ann? yes
          no

Ann is in the ___and.

yes	
yes	
ba**nd**	
hand	
c**an**	
taps	
pan	
t**a**ps	
tap	

Is this a band? yes
no

Is it in the sand? yes
no

This is a ba＿＿ in the sand.

Sam has a can in his hand.
sand.

Tap, tap! Sam taps on the c＿＿.

Tap, tap! Ann taps on a dish.
naps

Sam taps on a can.
pan.

Ann t＿＿ps on a pan.

Sam and Ann ＿＿ap on pans.

42

yes	 Tap, tap! Did the man tap? yes no
yes	Snap, snap! Did Nip snap? yes no
snap	Snap! I can tap. snap.
tapping	Tap, tap! Sam is tapping. snapping.

43

yes	Did Nip snap at that man? yes no Nip can sn __ p.
sn<u>a</u>p	
snapping	Nip is napping. snapping.
<u>s</u>naps	Nip __ naps at an ant.
no	Is Nip snapping? yes no
napping	Nip is napping. tapping.
<u>n</u>aps	Nip __ aps on his mat.
no	Is Ann snapping? yes no
no	Is Ann napping? yes no
tapp<u>ing</u>	Ann is tapp _____ on a can. **44**

	Sam has tan pants on.
no	Is Sam's hat tan? yes no

Sam has his hat / pants in his hand.

Nip snaps at Sam's pan. / pants.

pants	
pants	

Nip has the pans. / pants.

Is Nip fast? yes no

pants	
yes	

Sam has his p___nts.

Sam hit / hid the pants in a bag.

p<u>a</u>nts	
hid	

45

can	
c**an**	
fish	
yes	
sn**a**ps	
bag	
no	

Ann has a pan.
can.

Nip snaps at the c___ ___.

This is a big fish.
dish.

Snap!

Can the fish snap? yes
no

Snap!

The fish sn___ps at a can.

It snaps at a bag.
bat.

Snap!

Can the bag snap
at the fish? yes
no

46

an ant	This is an ant. / a mat.
<u>a</u>nt	 This __nt can sting.
sing	Sam and Ann can sing. / sting.
st<u>i</u>ng	I can sting. / I can st__ng a man.
sting	I can sing / sting Nip.
sti<u>ng</u>	 I can sti__ __ Tab.

47

Miss Pat	
sing	
no	

This is an ant.
Miss Pat.

Miss Pat can sing.
sting.

Can Miss Pat sting? yes
no

---

ant

This ___nt can sting.

---

yes
An ant

Did the ant sting Tab? yes
no

A cat
An ant can sting.

---

no
yes
nno

Can Sam sting? yes
no

Did that ant sting Sam? yes
no

Did Sam sting the ant? yes
no

48

fish	
fi<u>sh</u>	
yes	
fin	
<u>f</u>ish	
fins	
<u>fish</u>	
f<u>i</u>ns	

I am a dish.
      fish.

A fi __ __ has fins.

Is this a fish? yes
           no

It has a big fin.
          fan.

I am a __ish.

A fish has fins.
        pins.

This is a big f __ __ __ .

It has big f __ ns.

49

n<u>o</u>	
yes	
f<u>an</u>	
yes	
<u>sh</u>ip	
fish	
fins	
<u>f</u>ish	
<u>f</u>ins	

Is this a fin? yes
no

Is it a fan? yes
no

It is a tan f __ __.

Is this a ship? yes
no

It is Sam's __ __ip.

This is a fast fish.
ship.

A fish has fans.
fins.

Sam has a __ish.

The fish has __ins.

50

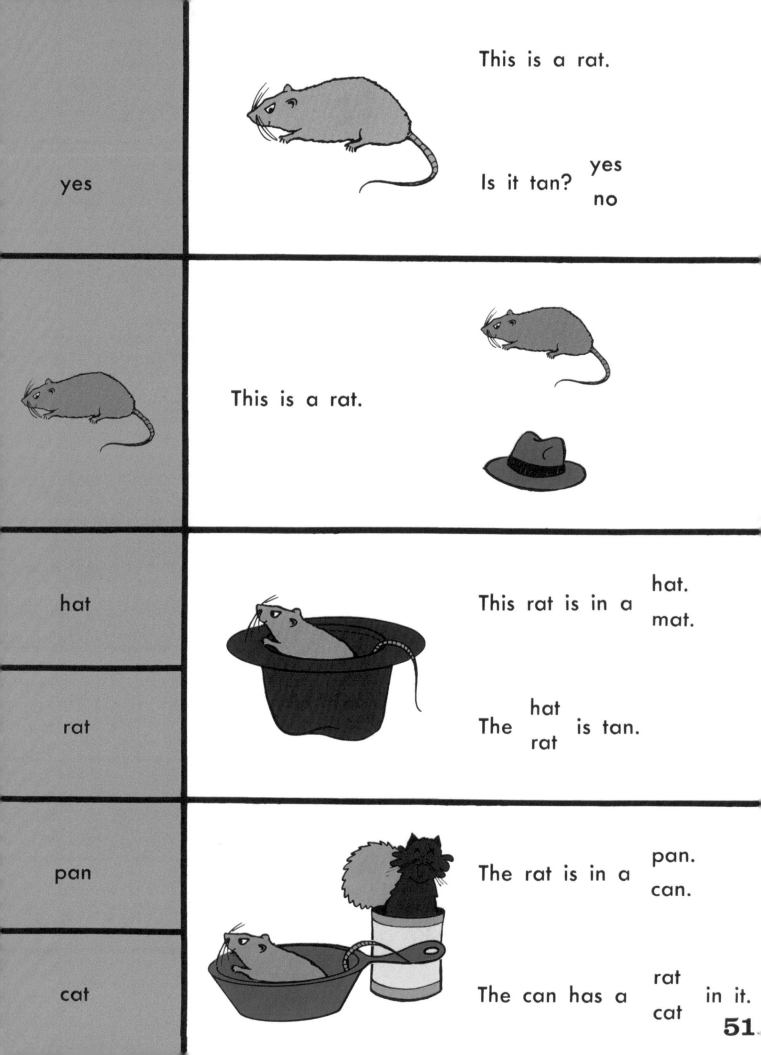

This is a rat.

Is it tan? yes
no

This is a rat.

This rat is in a hat.
mat.

The hat is tan.
rat

The rat is in a pan.
can.

The can has a rat in it.
cat

51

mat	
mat	

This is a ^rat.
mat.

It is a tan ___at.

cat	
ma**t**	
cat	

This is a ^cat.
rat.

The cat is on a ma___.

The ___at is tan.

hat	
yes	
hat	

This is a ^hat.
rat.

Is it on a mat? ^yes
no

The ___at is on a mat.

yes	
r**at**	
hat	
hat	

Is this a rat? ^yes
no

It is a fat r___t.

The rat has on a ^ham.
hat.

The ___at is tan.

cat	
no	
rat	
r**at**	
r**at**	
rat	

This is Tab.

Tab is a cat.
           rat.

Is this a cat? yes
                no

This is a rat.
           hat.

Tab sniffs the r___t.

Nip snaps at the r_____.

The ___at ran.

S**a**m	
ran	
ra**n**	

S___m ran.

Ann sat.
        ran.

Sam and Ann ra___.

cat
r**a**n

This cat ran.
        rat

It r___n fast.

rat
ran

This rat ran.
        hat

The rat ___an fast.

man
ra**n**
r**an**
Sam
ran

The pan ran.
        man

Nip ra___.

Tab r_____.

Nip, Tab, and the man ___an.

54

band	
band	 This is a hand. band. Sam is in the __and.
b**a**nd	 The b__nd ran.
sand	 Sam ran in the band. sand.
sand	Ann ran in the __and.
s**a**nd	The s__nd is tan.

no	Is this a rat? yes / no
	This is a rag.
yes	Is it a tan rag? yes / no
	This is a rag.
rat	Ann has a rat. / bat.
rag	Sam has a bag. / rag.
rat	The rat / rag is tan.
no	Is this rat in a bag? yes / no
yes	Is it on a rag? yes / no
_rag	This is a rat on a ___ag. **56**

rag	
r<u>a</u>g	
yes	
<u>r</u>ag	
bag	
yes	
rip	

Sam has a rat.
rag.

Sam can rip the r __ g.

Did Sam rip the rag? yes
no

The __ag has a rip in it.

Ann has a bag.
rag.

Can Ann rip the bag? yes
no

The bag has a rip
rat in it.

57

rag	
bag	
r<u>i</u>p	

The ^{bag} _{rag} is tan.

That is a rip in the ^{bag.} _{rag.}

The bag has a r___p in it.

---

rat	
hat	
mat	
<u>r</u>at	

This is a ^{rag.} _{rat.}

The rat has on a ^{hat.} _{cat.}

The rat is on a ^{map.} _{mat.}

The ___at is tan.

---

bat	
rag	

The ^{bat} _{rat} is in a bag.

The rat is on a ^{rag.} _{bag.}

---

rag	
<u>r</u>ipping	

Ann is ripping a ^{rag.} _{bag.}

Sam is ___ipping a bag.

58

can	 Sam trips on a can. / pan.
yes	Did that man trip? yes / no
tripping	Sam is ripping. / tripping.
p<u>a</u>n	 Sam trips on a p___n.
yes	 Is Ann tripping? yes / no
cat	Ann trips on the mat. / cat.

59

N**i**p	Tab ran past N__p.
ra**n**	Tab and Nip ra__ past Ann.
_ran	Tab, Nip, and Ann __an past Sam.
yes	Did Sam trip? yes no

60

no	
rat	
cat	
mat	
pan	
pan	
mat	

Am I a cat? yes
no

I am a rat.
rag.

I ran past a cat.
bat.

The cat is on a mat.
map.

I hid in a fan.
pan.

The cat ran past the __an.

I am napping on the cat's __at.

bat	
sand	
<u>s</u>and	
yes	
s<u>a</u>nd	
trips	

That is Sam's bat.
bag.

It is in the band.
sand.

Sam ran in the __and.

Did Sam trip on the bat? yes
no

Sam is in the s__nd.

Ann rips on Sam.
trips

62

snaps	 Nip **snaps / sniffs** at that man.
sniffs	 Tab **snaps / sniffs** at a can.
no	 Is Sam tripping? **yes / no**
no	Is Sam sitting? **yes / no**
yes	Is Sam standing? **yes / no**
<u>st</u>anding	Sam is ___tanding in the sand.
cat	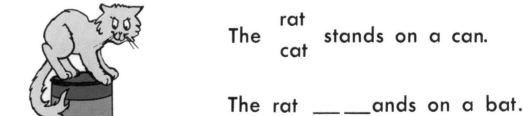 The **rat / cat** stands on a can.
<u>st</u>ands	The rat __ __ands on a bat.
rag	The ant stands on a **rag. / bag.**

63

can

The cat ran past a can. / pan.

ra<u>n</u>

Sam ra___ fast.

p<u>a</u>st

Sam ran p___st Ann.

fan

Nip ran past a fin. / fan.

<u>p</u>ast

Sam ran ___ast Nip.

sand	
napping	
taps	
Tab	
ran	

Tab is in the   sand.
             band.

Tab is   napping.
        tapping.

Miss Pat   naps   Tab.
           taps

Miss Pat ran past T___b.

Tab r___n fast.

• • •

65

mat	
m**at**	
Tab's	

Miss Pat is at Tab's
hat.
mat.

That is a rat on the m__ __.

That mat is
Nip's.
Tab's.

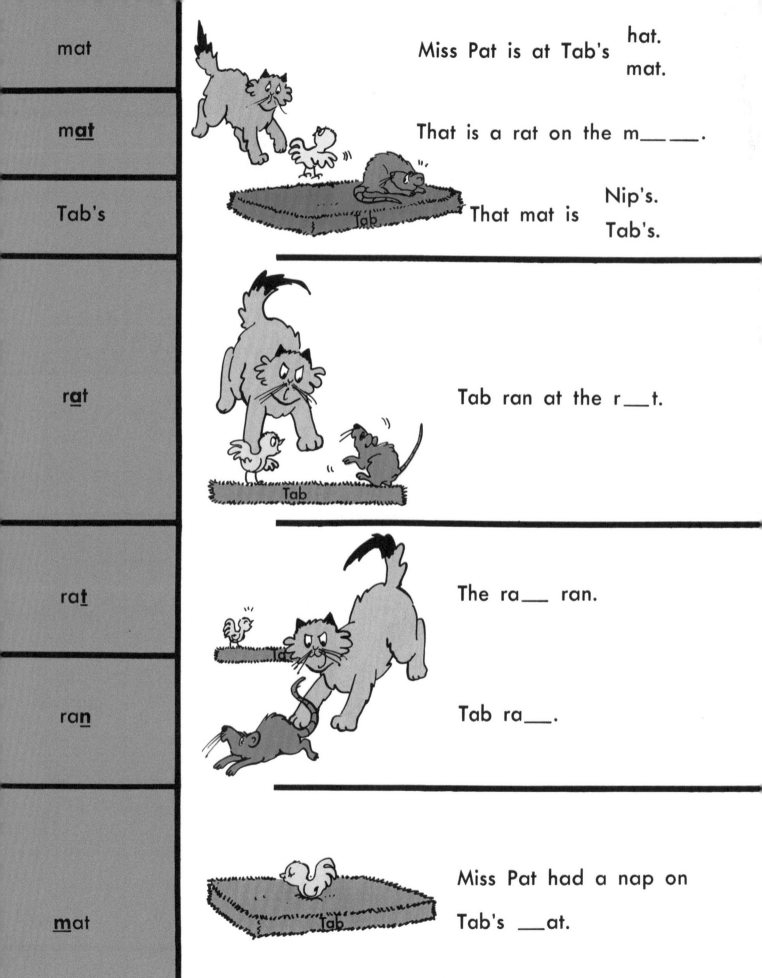

r**a**t	

Tab ran at the r__t.

ra**t**	
ra**n**	

The ra__ ran.

Tab ra__.

mat	

Miss Pat had a nap on

Tab's __at.

66

yes	
Pat	

Did Miss Pat sing? yes
no

Yes, Miss P____ ____ sang.

sat	
no	
sang	

Sam sat / sang in the sand.

Did Ann sit? yes
no

Ann sat. / sang.

This man sang.

sand	
sat	
sang	
sang	

Sam and Ann sat in the s____nd.

Sam s____t and sang.

Ann sat and s____ng.

Sam and Ann ____ang.

67

hat	
<u>tr</u>ips	Ann trips on Sam's bat. hat. Sam ___ ___ips on Ann's cat.
<u>h</u>at	This is Sam's __at.
<u>c</u>at	Tab is Ann's __at.
no	Is this a hat? yes no
no	Is it a cat? yes no
Th<u>is</u>	Th__s is a ring.
Ann'<u>s</u>	It is Ann'__ ring.

68

yes	
ring	
sting	
no	
sing	
r<u>i</u>ng	

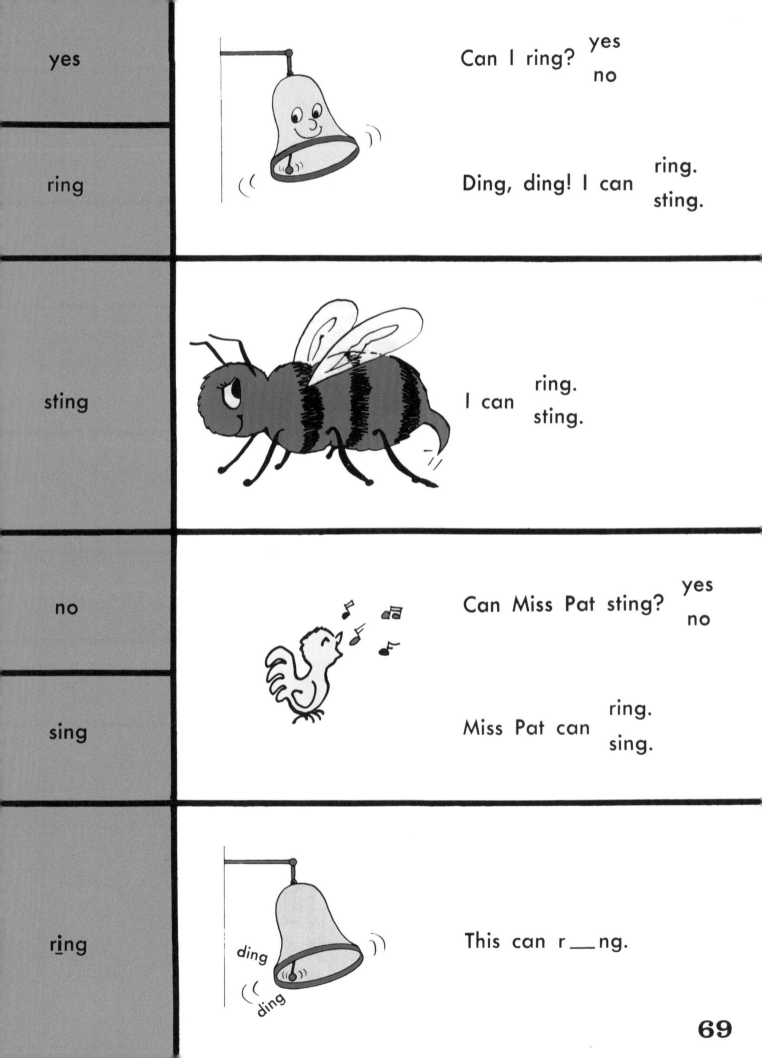

Can I ring? yes
no

Ding, ding! I can ring.
sting.

I can ring.
sting.

Can Miss Pat sting? yes
no

Miss Pat can ring.
sing.

ding
ding

This can r ___ ng.

69

sing	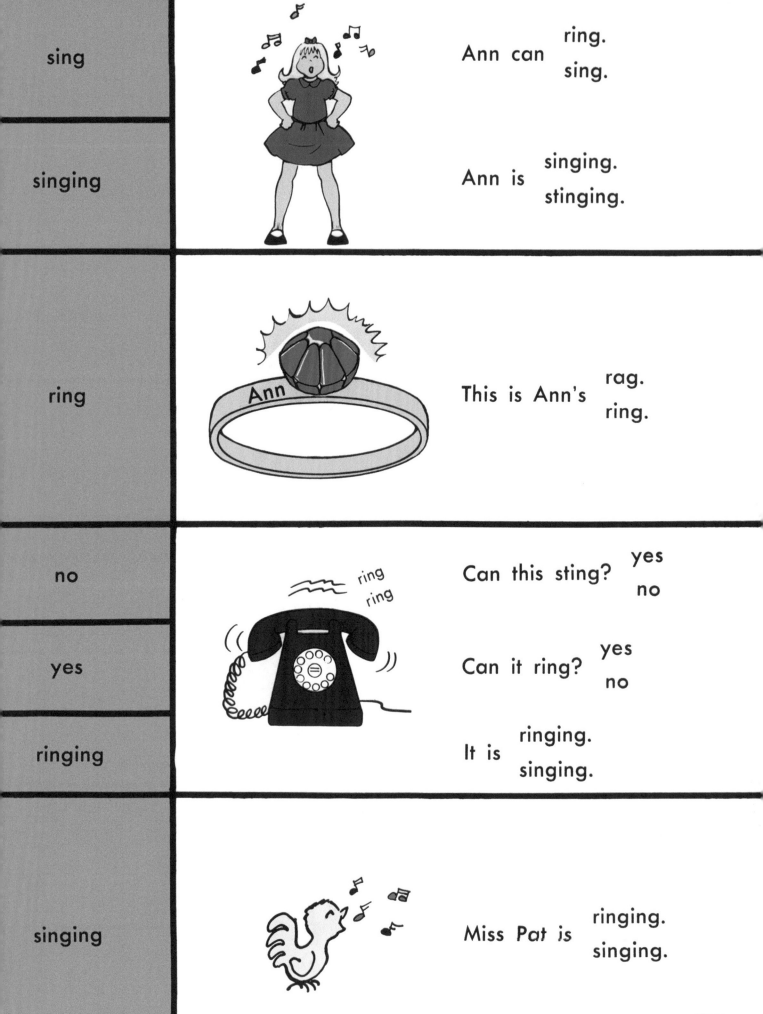 Ann can ring. / sing.
singing	Ann is singing. / stinging.
ring	This is Ann's rag. / ring.
no	Can this sting? yes / no
yes	Can it ring? yes / no
ringing	It is ringing. / singing.
singing	Miss Pat is ringing. / singing.

70

sang	
sa**ng**	Sam and Ann sang. / rang.
	Sam sang, and Ann sa ___ ___ .
yes	
	Did it ring? yes / no
rang	Yes, it sang. / rang.
ran	
	Sam ran. / rang.
ran	Ann ___an.
f**a**st	
	Sam is f___st.
p**a**st	Sam ran p___st Ann.
Sam	Sam / Ann has it.

71

TEST 2

Bang!   The bat hit the   pan.
                          mat.

The can hit the   pin.
                  pan.

Is Nip napping?   yes
                  no

Is Nip tapping?   yes
                  no

Nip is sn___pping at an ant.

Is Sam tripping?   yes
                   no

Sam is ripping a   rat.
                   rag.

The rag has a r___p in it.

That is a   cat   in the hat.
            rat

The   hat   is tan.
      rat

dripping

Drip, drip!   This is   ripping.
dripping.

yes

Is Nip dripping?   yes
no

dish

That is a fish in the d___sh.

dripping

The fish is   tripping.
dripping.

yes

Did Sam's pants drip?   yes
no

drip

The pants dr___p on Ann's hat.

73

fish	Sam has a dripping dish. / fish.
drips	The fish rips / drips on Nip.
dripping	Miss Pat is tripping. / dripping.
drips	Miss Pat ___rips on Ann.
ripping	Sam is ripping / dripping a rag.
dripping	This rag is tripping. / dripping.
drips	It ___ ___ips on a bag.

tripping	
yes	Ann is ripping. tripping. Did Ann trip on Sam? yes no
yes	Did Sam rip his pants? yes no
r**i**p	That is a r___p in his pants.
map	That is a mat map in Ann's hands.
ripping	Ann is tripping ripping the big map.
dripping	ripping. This is dripping. tripping.

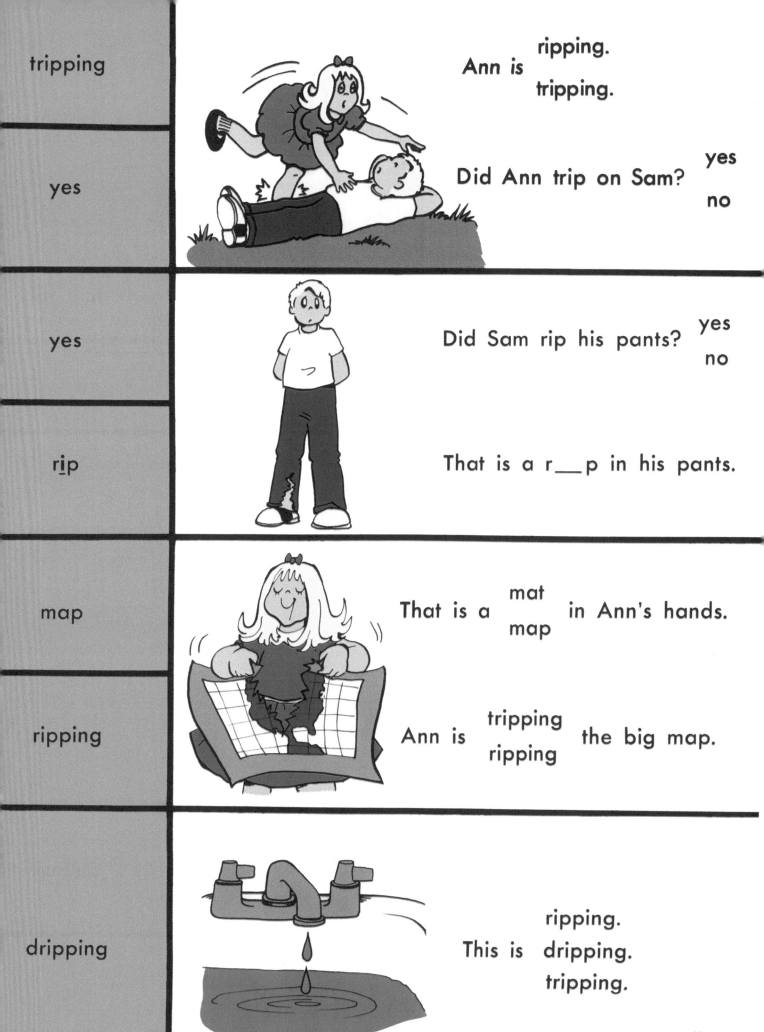

75

	Sam can print.
map	Sam prints on his mat. map.
yes	Can Ann print? yes no
no	Can Tab print? yes no
Ann	Ann Tab is printing.
can	Ann prints on a can. pan.
p**an**	Sam prints on a p__ __.
yes	Is Ann printing? yes no
yes	Is Sam printing? yes no
pr**i**nts	Ann pr__nts **Tab**.
prints	Sam __rints **Nip**. **76**

tapping		Ann is napping / tapping on a can.
tripping		Sam is tripping. / ripping.
trips		Sam tr__ps on a can.
dripping		Sam's hat is dripping. / ripping.
drips		It dr__ps on Tab.
ripping		Ann is tripping / ripping a rag.
rip		The rag has a __ip in it.

77

pig	This is a pin. / pig.
sand	It is in the sand. / band.
digging	The pig is digging. / dripping.
sa**nd**	Sam is in the sa___.
sitting	Sam is sitting. / standing.
yes	Is Sam printing? yes / no
printi**ng**	Sam is printi___ in the sand.
yes	Is Ann printing? yes / no
pr**i**nting	Ann is pr__nting in the sand.
pr**i**nting	Ann is ___inting **cat**.
fish	Nip is sniffing a fish. / dish.
sniffing	Tab is __ __iffing the fish.
dripp**ing**	The fish is drippi___.

pri<u>nt</u>	Sam can prin___.
yes	Can Ann print? yes no
pri<u>nt</u>	Sam and Ann can pri___ ___.

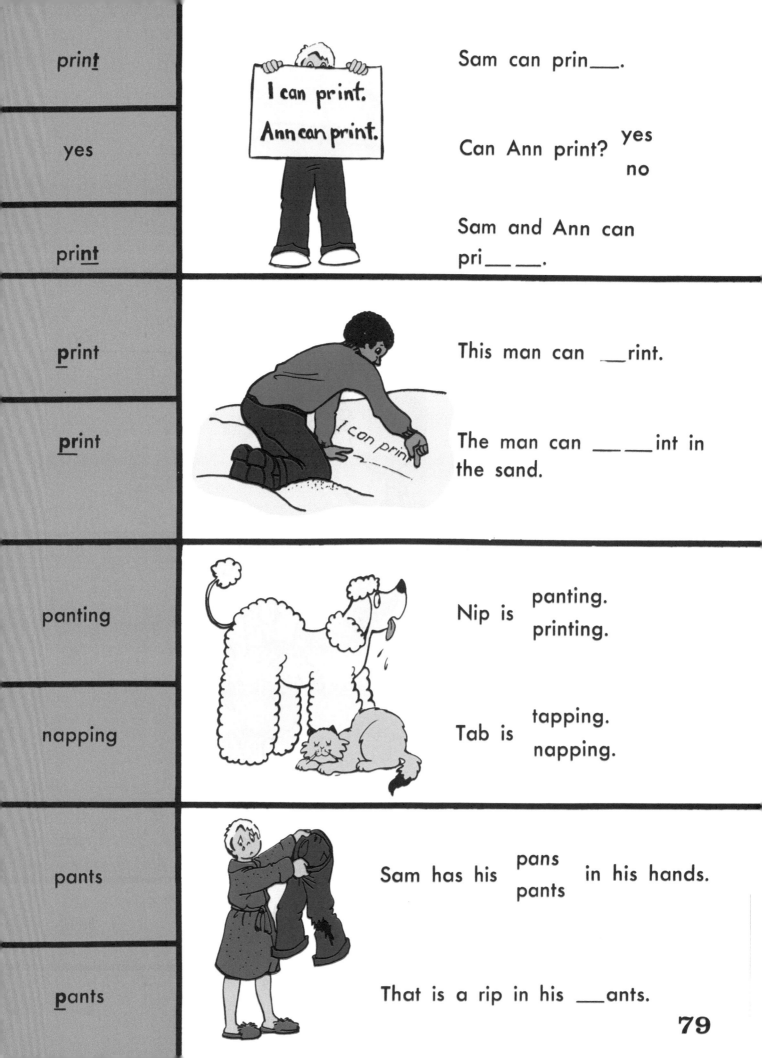

<u>p</u>rint	This man can ___rint.
<u>pr</u>int	The man can ___ ___int in the sand.

pan<u>ting</u>	Nip is panting. printing.
napping	Tab is tapping. napping.

pants	Sam has his pans pants in his hands.
<u>p</u>ants	That is a rip in his ___ants.

79

singing	Miss Pat is singing. / ringing.
hat	Miss Pat is on Ann's mat. / hat.
m<u>at</u>	Ann is on Tab's m__t.
m<u>at</u>	Tab's m__ __ is tan.
yes	Is Ann's hat tan? yes / no
napping	Tab is napping. / tapping.
bag	Tab is in a bag. / rag.
can	Nip is sniffing a cat. / can.
c<u>an</u>	The c__ __ has mints in it.
hands	Sam is standing on his hat. / hands.
rip	That is a pin / rip in his pants.
d<u>i</u>sh	A fish is in Nip's d__sh.
fi<u>sh</u>	The fi__ __ is dripping.
hat	It drips on Sam's rat. / hat.

80

pants	 Nip snaps at Sam's ~~pants.~~ hands.
ran	 Sam ~~rang~~ ran fast.
_r_an	Nip ___an fast.
bit	 Nip ~~bit~~ hit Sam's pants.
p_a_nts	That is a rip in Sam's p___nts.
yes	Is Sam sad? yes no

napping	 Nip is napping. snapping.
yes	
c<u>a</u>t	Is that a fat cat? yes no  The c__t ran past Nip.
c<u>at</u>	 A tan c_____ ran past Nip.
pa<u>st</u>	A thin cat ran pa_____ him.
ra<u>n</u>	Nip ra__ fast.
sand	 The cats sat in the sand. band.

yes	Is that an ant on Sam? yes / no
a**nt**	The a_____ is on Sam's chin.
ant	Sam has an ___nt on his chin.
no	Did this man hit his hand? yes / no
yes	Did the man hit his chin? yes / no
yes	Did Sam trip? yes / no
hit	Sam hit / bit his chin.

83

chin		This man has a big pin. chin.
ch<u>i</u>n		This is Sam's ch___n.
fins		A fish has fins. chins.
dripping		Ann's chin is tripping. dripping.

yes	Is this a man? yes / no
m<u>an</u>	This m____ is rich.
yes	Is this man rich? yes / no
r<u>i</u>ch	This is a r___ch man.
no	Is this a rich man? yes / no
yes	Am I rich? yes / no
<u>r</u>ich	I am a ___ich man.

85

can	
c**an**	
yes	
h**a**nds	
no	
Sam	
can	
chin	

That is a tin cat.
That is a tin can.

Sam can catch the c___ ___.

Did Sam catch the can? yes
no

It is in his h___nds.

Did Ann catch the can? yes
no

The can hit Ann.
The can hit Sam.

It hit his hand.
It hit his chin.

86

can	Ann is catching a can. pan.
pan	Sam is catching a _____.
yes	Can a cat catch a rat? yes no
rat	Tab can catch a _____.
c<u>a</u>tch	Sam can c___tch Nip.
cat<u>ch</u>	Ann can cat_____ Tab.
yes	Can a man catch a fish? yes no
<u>c</u>atching	This man is ___atching a big fish.

87

r<u>a</u>t	
trap	
tr<u>a</u>p	
tra<u>p</u>	
<u>t</u>rap	
rat	
<u>tr</u>ap	

This is a rat trap.

It can catch a r___t.

A rat is at the   trap.
                    trip.

The rat sniffs the tr___p.

Snap!   The rat is
in the tra___.

A ___rap can catch a rat.

Sam has the   rat.
                trap.

Ann has the _____ap.

sitting	
hat	
A**nn**	
yes	
f**a**st	
h**at**	
hat	
dripping	
dripp**ing**	

Ann is standing / sitting in the sand.

Ann has on a tan hat. / mat.

Sam ran past A___ ___.

Did Sam hit Ann's hat? yes / no

Sam ran f___st.

Sam can catch the h___ ___.

Sam has Ann's ___ ___ ___.

The hat is dripping. / tripping.

Sam is dripp___ ___ ___.

89

hat	Sam hands Ann the ___ ___ ___ .
sand	Ann sits in the s___nd.
fish	The hat had a fish / dish in it.
yes	Did Sam catch a fish in Ann's hat? yes / no
catching	The man is c___tching a fish.
yes	Did Ann catch a fish? yes / no
catch	Tab can ___atch a rat.
catch	Nip can cat___ ___ Tab.

90

no	 Is this man rich? yes no
yes	
ri**ch**	This is a ri____ man.
an ant	 That is an ant on the man. a hat
chin	The ant is on his hand. chin.
ant	That ___nt can sting.
yes	 Did the ant sting the man? yes no Did it sting his chin? yes no
yes	

rip	That is a rip / trip in Sam's pants.
p**a**nts	Sam hands Ann his p__nts.
pants	Ann can patch the __ants.
pant**s**	That is a patch on Sam's pant__.
p**a**t**ch**	The p__tch is tan.
yes	Did Ann patch the pants? yes / no
yes	Is this a man's hat? yes / no
yes	Is that a patch on it? yes / no
pa**tch**	The pat____ is tan. **92**

no	Is this a patch? yes / no
no	Is it a mat? yes / no
Th**i**s	Th___s is a match.
match	This man has a mat. / match.
match	The ___atch is in his hand.
mat	This is a mat. / match.
patch	The mat has a pat / patch on it.
pat**ch**	The pat_____ is tan.
match	That is a match / patch on the mat.
match	An ant is standing on the mat. / match.
mat**ch**	The mat___ is tan.

93

fi̱sh	
cat**ch**	
no	

Sam can catch a f__sh.

Ann can cat___ a fish.

Did Tab catch a fish?　yes　no

cat	
c**at**	

This is a　cat.　rat.

A c___ can scratch.

yes

Did Sam catch a cat?　yes　no

yes

Did the cat scratch Sam?　yes　no

chin

Sam has a scratch on his　chin.　fin.

94

yes	
scr**a**tch	
hand	
scratch	
match	
mat**ch**	
ti**n**	
patch	
no	

Can Tab scratch? yes
no

Cats can scr___tch.

This is Sam's band.
hand.

Sam has a patch on
scratch
his hand.

That is a match on the can.
scratch

The mat___ ___ is tan.

The can is tin.
tan.

Sam has a match on
patch
his pants.

Is the patch tan? yes
no

95

yes	 Can a cat scratch? yes / no
scr<u>a</u>tch	That cat can scr___tch a man.
ch<u>i</u>n	 It is scratching his ch___n.
no	 Did a rat scratch this man? yes / no
yes	Did a cat scratch him? yes / no
scratch	The man has a patch / scratch on his chin.
scra<u>tch</u>	
<u>s</u>cratch	That cat can scrat___.

I can scratch.

It can ___cratch Nip.

96

no	Did Ann catch the can? yes no
yes	Did Sam catch it? yes no
no	Is the cat scratching Ann? yes no
yes	Is it scratching Sam? yes no
patch	That is a patch match on Sam's hat.
scr<u>a</u>tch	That is a scr___tch on his chin.
no	Is that a patch on Ann's chin? yes no
no	Is it a match? yes no
yes	Is it a scratch? yes no

97

yes	Is this Miss Pat? yes no
scratching	Miss Pat is catching in the sand. scratching
scr<u>a</u>tch	Miss Pat can scr___tch.
an ant	Miss Pat has an ant. a cat.
yes	Did Miss Pat catch it? yes no
cat<u>ch</u>	Miss Pat can cat___ ___ an ant.
scratching	This man is catching his chin. scratching
scrat<u>ch</u>	A man can scrat___ ___ his chin.
no	Is Nip catching an ant? yes no
no	Is Nip scratching Ann? yes no
scratch<u>ing</u>	Nip is scratch___ ___ ___ his chin.

98

no	This is Kit. Is Kit a pig? yes **no**
no	Is Kit a fish? yes no
Kit	Ann has Kit. Nip.
K<u>i</u>t	K__t is a kitten.
yes	Is this Kit? yes no
yes	Is Kit a kitten? yes no

This is a kitten.

99

mat	Tab and Kit sit on a mat. / hat.
Ki**t**	Ki___ is a kitten.
c**a**t	Tab is a c___t.
yes	Can Tab scratch? yes / no
scrat**ch**	Kit can scrat___ ___.
scratch	Cats and kittens can ___ ___ratch.
digging	Kit is digging. / sniffing.
di**g**	Kittens can di___.
napping	Kit is panting. / napping.
K**i**ttens	K___ttens can nap.

100

no	
Ann's	
yes	
Sam's	
mitten	
yes	
kitten	

Is this a kitten? yes
                   no

This is a mitten.

It is Ann's
       Sam's   mitten.

Is this a mitten? yes
                   no

This mitten is Ann's.
                Sam's.

It is Sam's mitten.
             kitten.

Is this Kit? yes
              no

Kit is a mitten.
          kitten.

This is a mitten.

101

yes	
no	
k<u>i</u>tten	
m<u>i</u>tten	
Ann'<u>s</u>	
k<u>i</u>tten	
m<u>i</u>tten	
kitten	
<u>m</u>itten	

Is this Kit? yes
no

Is Kit a mitten? yes
no

Kit is a k___tten.

Kit has a m___tten.

That is Ann'___ mitten.

The k___tten is in
the m___tten.

Sam has the kitten.
mitten.

Ann has the ___itten.

mitten	Tab has Ann's kitten. mitten.
m̲itten	Tab brings Ann the __itten.
r̲ing	Sam has Ann's r__ng.
h̲and	The ring is in Sam's h__nd.
r̲ing	Sam brings Ann the __ing.
ship	Ann has Sam's fish. ship.
sh̲ip	Ann is bringing Sam the ___ip.

103

dish	
h**a**nds	

Ann brings Kit a   dish.
                   fish.

The dish is in Ann's h＿＿ nds.

di**sh**	
pr**i**nts	

Ann prints on the di＿＿ ＿＿ .

Ann pr＿＿ nts a **k**.

yes	
Kit'**s**	

Did Ann print **Kit**
on the dish?   yes
               no

That is Kit'＿＿ dish.

d**ish**	
fi**sh**	

Kit has the d＿＿ ＿＿ ＿＿ .

Sam is bringing
Kit a fi＿＿ ＿＿ .

104

singing	 Ann is singing. ringing.
ringing	This is ringing. bringing.
bringing	 Ann is ringing bringing Sam his bat.
bringing	Sam is __ringing Ann a hat.
rag	 Nip brings Sam a rag. bag.
brings	Tab __ __ings Ann a bag.

f**a**st	
p**a**st	
yes	
kitten	
kitten	
br**i**ngs	
brings	
br**i**ngs	

Kit ran f___st.

Kit ran p___st Tab.

Did Tab catch Kit? yes no

Tab has the kitten. mitten.

Kit is Tab's ___itten.

Tab br___ngs the kitten to Ann.

Ann ___rings a dish to Tab.

Sam ___ ___ings a fish to Kit.

106

Sam	Nip ran to Ann. Sam.
A**nn**	Tab ran to A ___ ___.
ra**n**	Kit ra___ to Tab.
sang	Ann sang rang to Sam.
pan	The cat ran to the can. pan.
rat	The cat rat ran to the can.
rat	The cat and the ___ ___ ___ ran.

107

TEST 3

Ann's hat / bat is dripping.

It drips / trips on a mat.

Is this man rich? yes / no

This man has a match / patch on his pants.

The pat___ ___ is tan.

Can cats scratch? yes / no

This cat is catching / scratching a man.

It is scratching his hand. / chin.

Is Kit a mitten? yes / no

Kit is a k___tten.

sitting	
hat	
yes	
singing	
no	
catching	
yes	
sand	
mitten	
mitten	
kitten	
bringing	

Sam is sitting / singing in the sand.

Sam has a big h___ ___ on.

Is Ann singing? yes no

Ann is sing___ ___ ___ to Sam.

Is Tab in the sand? yes no

Tab is patching / catching a fish.

Is Kit in the sand? yes no

Kit is scratching in the s___ ___ ___ .

Tab has a mitten. / kitten.

Tab is bringing the ___itten to Sam.

Sam has a k___tten.

Sam is bring___ ___ ___ the kitten to Ann.

109

yes	
sting	
Sam	
kitten	
Kit	
hands	
pants	
pin	
pin	

Did the ant sting the kitten? yes no

That ant can sing. sting.

Kit ran to Sam. Ann.

Kit is a sad k___tten.

Sam has K_____ in his hands.

Kit fits in Sam's ___ands.

Sam has a rip in his hat. pants.

Ann has a pin. pan.

Ann is bringing the p___ to Sam.

110

no	Is this a kitten? yes no
no	This is a kitchen. Is Ann in the kitchen? yes no
yes	Is this Kit? yes no
kitten	Kit is a kitten. kitchen.
yes	Is this a kitchen? yes no
mitten	That is a kitten mitten in the kitchen.
yes	Is Ann in the kitchen? yes no
pan	Ann has a pin. pan.

111

no	 Is Sam in the kitchen? yes / no
sand	Sam is in the sand. / band.
yes	 Is Miss Pat in the kitchen? yes / no
kitchen	Kit is in the __itchen.
yes	Is Kit's dish in the kitchen? yes / no

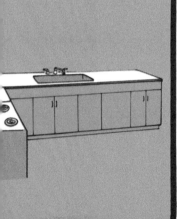 This is a kitchen.

kitchen	 This man has a big kitchen. / kitten.
yes	Is the man in his kitchen? yes / no

112

h**a**nd	Sam has a tack. The tack is in his h___nd.
yes t**a**ck	Is this a tack? yes no It is a tan t___ck.
Ann no h**a**s t**a**n	Ann Sam has a tack. Is the tack tan? yes no Sam h___s a sack. The sack is t___n.
no yes	Is this a tack? yes no Is it a sack? yes no

113

tack	That is a tack / sack on the can.
cat	The sack has a cat / can in it.
sack	The tack / sack is tan.
yes	Is this Nip? yes no
no	Is Nip in a sack? yes no
Ni**p**	N___ ___ is on his back.
no	Is this man in a sack? yes no
back	This man is on his bat. / back.
yes	Is Sam on his back? yes no

back	Sam had an ant on his chin. back.
b<u>a</u>ck	Ann hit the ant on Sam's b__ck.
sack	This man has a tack. sack.
s<u>a</u>ck	The s__ck is on his back.
no	Is this a back? yes no
tack	It is a tack. sack.
rat	The cat rat is on its back.
sack	The cat is in the tack. sack.
<u>s</u>ack	The __ack is tan. **115**

sack	
sa<u>ck</u>	

Nip has a tack / sack on his back.

The sa____ has sand in it.

sand	
yes	

Sam is in the sack. / sand.

Is Sam on his back?　yes / no

sack	
sack	
no	

That is a sack / tack in the sand.

The cat is in the sand. / sack.

Is the sack tan?　yes / no

no	
cat	
b<u>a</u>ck	

Is this pig on its back?　yes / no

That is a can / cat on the pig.

The pig has a cat on its b__ck.

116

kitten	This is a kitten. / mitten.
back	The kitten is on its back. / sack.
tack	That is an ant on the tack. / sack.
ta<u>ck</u>	The ta___ ___ is tan.
sack	Ann has a sack. / tack.
ta<u>ck</u>	Sam has a ta___ ___.
b<u>a</u>ck	Nip is on his b___ck.
b<u>a</u>ck	Tab sat on Nip's b___ck.
ba<u>ck</u>	Nip has a cat on his ba___ ___.

117

no	Is this Sam's chin? yes no
no	Is it his back? yes no
hand	This is Sam's band. hand.
fin	This fish has a big pin. fin.
back	The fin is on its band. back.
yes	Is that an ant on Sam? yes no
chin	The ant is on Sam's fin. chin.
yes	Did this man trip? yes no
chin	The man hit his ch___n.

catch	
<u>c</u>atching	Nip can patch / catch Ann's hat.
	Nip is __atching the hat.
hat	Nip brings the _ _ _ _ back to Ann.
b<u>a</u>ck	That is Kit on Ann's b__ck.
sand	Ann is in the sand. / sack.
<u>s</u>ack	Tab is in the s__ck.
tack	Sam has a sack. / tack.
ta<u>ck</u>	The ta__ __ is in his hand.
<u>s</u>ack	That is a __ack in Ann's hands.
sa<u>ck</u>	The sa__ __ has sand in it.

fishing	
yes	
fi<u>sh</u>	
yes	
cat<u>ch</u>	
f<u>i</u>sh	
yes	

Sam is   napping.
          fishing.

Did Sam catch
a fish?   yes
          no

Tab has Sam's fi___ ___ .

Did Nip catch Tab?   yes
                     no

Nip can cat___ ___ a cat.

Sam has the f___sh back.

Did Nip bring it
to him?   yes
          no

• • •

120

yes	Is Ann in the kitchen? yes no
h**a**nd	That is a pan in Ann's h___nd.
k**i**tchen	Sam is in the k___tchen.
hands	Sam has a fish in his ___ands.
fish	Sam hands the f_____ to Ann.
p**an**	The fish is in the p_____ .
h**a**nds	The pan is in Ann's h___nds.
k**i**tchen	Ann is in the k___tchen.
kitchen	And Sam is in the ___itchen.

121

rag	
b<u>a</u>ck	
rat	

The cat has a rat / rag on its back.

The rat has an ant on its b___ck.

The rat / rag is tan.

sack	
sa<u>ck</u>	
<u>s</u>and	

This man has a tack / sack on his back.

The sa___ ___ has sand in it.

The ___and is tan.

sack	
ba<u>ck</u>	

Nip is sniffing a back. / sack.

That is a cat on Nip's ba___ ___.

sand	
mat<u>ch</u>	
ta<u>ck</u>	
a<u>nt</u>	

The match is in the sand. / sack.

That is a tack on the mat___ ___.

An ant is on the ta___ ___.

The a___ ___ is tan. **122**

no	Is that a cat in the sack? yes no
sa<u>ck</u>	That is a chicken. The chicken is in the sa __ __ .
no	Is this a kitten? yes no
yes	Is it a chicken? yes no
no	Is this a kitten? yes no
kitchen	It is a kitchen. chicken.

This is a chicken.

123

chicken	
kit**te**n	
chicken	
yes	
sand	
sa**nd**	
catching	
scratching	
scratch**ing**	
ch**in**	

Sam has a   kitten.
              chicken.

Ann has a kitt____ .

The   kitten   is tan.
      chicken

Is this a chicken?   yes
                    no

It is in the   band.
              sand.

A chicken can scratch
in the sa____ .

Sam is   catching   a chicken.
        scratching

The chicken is   catching   Sam.
            scratching

It is scratch_____ Sam's chin.

Sam has a scratch
on his ch____ .

124

patch	That is a patch / *match* on Sam's pants.
pat**ch**	The pat____ is tan.
match	This man has a mat. / match.
mat**ch**	The mat____ is in his hand.
trap	This is a rat trip. / trap.
catch	A trap can match / catch a rat.
chicken	This is a kitchen. / chicken.
chicken	This ____icken is in the sand.
yes	Is the chicken scratching? yes / no
scrat**ch**	A chicken can scrat____ in the sand. **125**

yes	
no	
yes	
<u>ch</u>icken	
no	
hid	
sack	
ch<u>i</u>cken	
s<u>a</u>ck	

Is this a chicken? yes
no

Is it in the kitchen? yes
no

Did Nip snap at
the chicken? yes
no

The ___ ___icken ran.

Did Nip catch the chicken? yes
no

The chicken hid.
hit.

It hid in a sack.
tack.

Sam has the ch___cken.

Nip has the s___ck.

126

tan	
chick**en**	
no	
kitch**en**	
no	
kitt**en**	
no	
mitt**en**	

This chicken is tin.
tan.

It is a big tan chick_____.

Is this a chicken? yes
no

This is a kitch_____.

Is this a kitchen? yes
no

It is a kitt_____.

Is this a kitten? yes
no

It is a mitt_____.

127

cat	Sam has a cat / hat on his lap.
Sam's	The cat sits on Sam'___ lap.
hat	This man has a tan mat. / hat.
lap	The hat is on his lap. / map.
Ann's	A kitten sat on Sam's / Ann's lap.
lap	That is a chicken on Sam's l___p.
no	Is that a cat on Sam's lap? yes / no
lap	Sam has a rat on his la___.

128

sack

lap

This is a man's lap.

no

man's

lips

yes

That is a tack on
          sack
Ann's lap.

Sam has a bat on
his __ap.

Is this a man's lap?   yes
                       no

This is a m___n's lip.

Sam has lips.

Sam can lick his l__ps.

Is Sam licking his lips?   yes
                           no   **129**

bag	Sam has a big bag. rag.
ba<u>g</u>	The b__ __ has mints in it.
mi<u>nt</u>	Sam hands Nip a mi__ __.
m<u>i</u>nt	Nip has the m__ nt.
mi<u>nt</u>	Nip licks the m__ __ __.
fish	Tab licks a fish. dish.
<u>l</u>icks	Nip __icks his dish.
li<u>ck</u>	A man can li__ __ his lips.
<u>l</u>ips	This man is licking his __ips.

130

bag	
b<u>a</u>g	
rag	
r<u>a</u>g	

Sam has a bag. rag.

It is a pink b__ g.

Ann has a rat. rag.

It is a pink r__ g.

This bag is pink.

yes	
no	
p<u>i</u>g	

Is this a pig? yes no

Is it tan? yes no

This p__ g is pink.

yes	
no	
bag	
r<u>at</u>	

Is this a rat? yes no

Is it pink? yes no

This r____ is tan. **131**

tan	 Sam has a tan / pink pig.
pink	Ann has a ___ink pig.
pink	Ann has p___nk lips.
	This man has pink lips.  
pan	 Sam has a fan and a pin. / pan.
yes	Is the pan pink? yes / no
pink	The fan is pink, and the pan is pi___ ___. **132**

lap	Nip sat on Sam's lip. lap.
l**a**p	Tab sat on Ann's l__p.
yes	Did Sam trip? yes no
lip	Sam hit his lip. lap.
ham	Sam sniffs the hat. ham.
l**i**ps	Sam licks his l__ps.
l**i**ps	Nip is licking his __ips.
yes	Can Nip sniff the ham? yes no
yes	Can a cat lick a kitten? yes no
licking	Tab is __icking the kitten.

This chicken is pink.

dish

yes

p<u>i</u>nk

This is a dish.
fish.

Is it pink? yes
no

This is a p___nk dish.

yes

no

<u>d</u>ish

Is this a dish? yes
no

Is it pink? yes
no

This ___ish is red.

dish

d<u>ish</u>

f<u>ish</u>

yes

Ann has a dish.
fish.

The d_ _ _ _ is red.

Sam has a f_ _ _ _.

Is the fish red? yes
no **134**

back	
sa<u>ck</u>	
tack	
<u>t</u>ack	
no	
ant	
band	
yes	
r<u>e</u>d	
<u>can</u>	
p<u>an</u>	
r<u>e</u>d	

This man has a sack
on his   bat.
             back.

The sa_ _ _ is red.

That ant is on a   tack.
                     sack.

The t_ _ _ _ _ is red.

Is the ant red?   yes
                  no

The _ _ _ _ is tan.

This man is in the   sand.
                     band.

Is his hat red?   yes
                  no

This man has a red hat
and r_ _d pants.

Ann has a pan and a c_ _ _.

The p_ _ is red.

The can is r_ _ _.

135

yes	 This is a bed. Is it red? yes no
yes	Is this a bed? yes no
no	Is it red? yes no
pink	This is a tan bed. pink
yes	Is this man in bed? yes no
yes	Is the bed red? yes no
r<u>e</u>d	The man has a r___d bed.
yes	 Is Sam in bed? yes no
b<u>e</u>d	Sam's b___d is red.
no	Is Nip in Sam's bed? yes no **136**

This is a bed.

This bed is red.

kitten

Kit is a chicken.
        kitten.

mitten

Kit has a kitchen.
         mitten.

mitten

The kitten is red.
     mitten

mittens

Ann has kittens on.
         mittens

pink

Ann has red mittens.
         pink

mittens

Sam has ___ittens on.

red

Sam has r___d mittens.

137

yes	Did Sam sit on his bed? yes no
b<u>e</u>d	Sam's b___d is red.
lap	Tab sat on Sam's lip. / lap.
red	Sam has a red / pink bed.
b<u>e</u>d	Nip sat on Sam's b__d.
<u>b</u>ed	Tab sat on Ann's __ed.
b<u>ed</u>	Ann has a pink b___ ___.
cat	Ann has a red cat. / hat.
fish	Sam has a fish. / dish.
f<u>ish</u>	Sam's f___ ___ ___ is red.
dish	Nip has a red dish. / fish.
d<u>ish</u>	Nip licks his d___ ___ ___.

138

no	Is this a hat? yes / no
	This is a dress.
yes	Is it red? yes / no
no	Is this dress red? yes / no
yes	Is this a pink dress? yes / no
yes	Is this a dress? yes / no
no	Is it red? yes / no
no	Is it pink? yes / no
tan	This dress is tin. / tan.
hat	Ann has on a red hat. / mat.
yes	Is Ann's dress red? yes / no
red	Ann has on a r__d dress. **139**

This is a dress.

yes

Is this a dress? yes
no

dr<u>e</u>ss

This is Ann's best dr___ss.

pink

Ann's best dress is red.
pink.

yes

Is this a dress? yes
no

no

Is it Ann's best dress? yes
no

<u>d</u>ress

This ___ress has rips in it.

dress

Ann has on the pink hat.
dress.

dr<u>ess</u>

It is Ann's best dre___ ___.

140

dress	 Nip has Ann's best dish. dress.
catching	 Sam is catching scratching Nip.
dr<u>e</u>ss	 Sam has Ann's dr__ss.
dr<u>ess</u>	Sam brings the dre____ to Ann.
	This is Ann's best dress.  

141

b**e**st	 This *man has* his best hat on. His b__st hat is tan.
best	 Ann's __est dress is pink.
fish **fish** **f**ish	 Sam has a big dish. fish. Ann has a thin f____ ___ ___. Sam has the best ___ish.
tan sa**ck** r**e**d **b**est	 The tan sack is the best. Sam has a tin sack. tan Ann has a pink sa___ ___ and a r___d sack. Sam's sack is the ___est.

yes	Is this a bed? yes no
yes	Is it red? yes no
<u>r</u>ed	It is a __ed bed.

That   hat   /   ham   is red.

Is the dress red?   yes   no

The dr__ss is pink.

| hat |
| no |
| dr<u>e</u>ss |

Is this pig red?   yes   no

It is a pink p____.

The pig is in the   sand.   /   sack.

| no |
| p<u>ig</u> |
| sand |

Sam's red pants   drip.   /   trip.

The pants drip on Ann's   hat.   /   dress.

That is Ann's best dre____.

| drip |
| dress |
| dre<u>ss</u> |

143

TEST 4

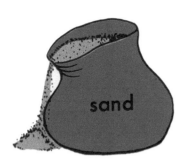

sand

This is a $\begin{array}{l}\text{sack.}\\ \text{tack.}\end{array}$

Is it red? $\begin{array}{l}\text{yes}\\ \text{no}\end{array}$

The sa___ has sand in it.

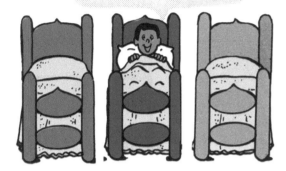

This is the best bed.

Is that man in bed? $\begin{array}{l}\text{yes}\\ \text{no}\end{array}$

The man is in a red___.

The $\begin{array}{l}\text{tan}\\ \text{red}\end{array}$ bed is the best.

This is a kitchen.

Sam has a $\begin{array}{l}\text{kitten.}\\ \text{chicken.}\end{array}$

The chicken is on his $\begin{array}{l}\text{lip.}\\ \text{lap.}\end{array}$

Sam is patting the ___icken.

144